# PRAYING
## *with* Mary

Mary Ford-Grabowsky

PARACLETE PRESS
BREWSTER, MASSACHUSETTS

*For my Beloved Christian, Helen, and Ryan,
who love learning and love God.*

*Praying with Mary*

2012 First Printing

Copyright © 2012 by Mary Ford-Grabowsky

ISBN: 978-1-61261-137-2 (Pack of five)

The Library of Congress has catalogued the original book *The Way of Mary*, from which this book is excerpted, as follows:

The way of Mary: following her footsteps toward God / by Mary Ford-Grabowsky.
    p. cm.
    Includes bibliographical references (p.     ) and index.
    ISBN 978-1-55725-522-8 (alk. paper)
1. Mary, Blessed Virgin, Saint—Prayers and devotions. I. Title.
BX2160.23.F67 2007
232.91—dc22                                    2007034938

10 9 8 7 6 5 4 3 2 1

Published by Paraclete Press
Brewster, Massachusetts
www.paracletepress.com

Printed in the United States of America

# CONTENTS

INTRODUCTION
5

ONE
*The Mother of Jesus*
11

TWO
*Following Mary's Footsteps
Toward God*
17

AFTER YOU READ
THIS BOOK
67

CREDITS
71

NOTES
73

# INTRODUCTION

In 1994, MY HUSBAND AND I SPENT AN amazing week in Guatemala with our daughter Tara, a medical student who was working in Guatemala City that summer in a hospital for the poor. Friends of hers recommended a visit to a village virtually unknown to tourists at the time: Chichicastenango. We rented an ancient Jeep for the drive up a wildly winding mountain road that was continually punctuated by giant potholes and deep ruts. Today it is a beautifully paved road, but on that day, I tried to avert my eyes from thousand-foot drops at every turn as we crashed into and out of a dozen ruts and eventually arrived at the top, totally unprepared for the breathtaking beauty all around us.

On one side, an ocean of Mayans dressed in bright blue and red were gathered for market day. On the other side, an alluring path led us to what appeared to be a tiny white church built on top of an ancient pyramid. At the top of the stairs, a very old Mayan *brujo* (healer) with a saintly face and stooped shoulders was gently swinging incense over a crippled woman, softly chanting prayers in his native Quiché. After a few minutes, the woman left, and the *brujo*, with an air of infinite peace and humility, opened the small doors of the church and humbly stationed himself at the back.

People who looked very poor and very ill waited in a long line for him.

Through the opened doors I saw in the semi-darkness a long row of burning white candles running the length of the center aisle floor, which was thickly covered with fresh flower petals. The beauty was beyond anything I had ever seen. My daughter and I tiptoed into the church and sat down on a side bench to be as unobtrusive as possible. I immediately felt myself saturated in love. The whole room was full of love. The air was rich and dense and luminous. I noticed beside me at the end of our bench a statue of Mary, unusually compelling in a tasteful combination of Mayan and Christian dress. It had a strong spiritual presence, as works of art portraying Mary often do, and I recited the Hail Mary. Everything seemed to slow down and stop. I could feel myself sinking deeper and deeper into beauty, into holiness. Before long, I lost track of time and even of myself.

My daughter nudged me, pointing to her watch. A half hour had gone by, and we had to check into the hotel. Reluctantly, I stood up to leave. Many years of prayer and meditation had given me wondrous experiences, spiritual and mystical, but the depths of love in this sacred place surpassed everything. Still enveloped in love, I listened to the Mayan's tender chanting for the poorest of the poor, then looked back at Mary, thinking about the power that she (and he) exuded.

Two days later, we drove down the mountain early for an appointment with a surgeon who would tell me the fate of a finger on my right hand. It had been nearly severed a few days earlier when a huge wrought-iron door had slammed on it, and it was not healing. The skin had turned black; the graft was not taking; and the doctor was not optimistic.

Suddenly I realized I had missed a once-in-a-lifetime opportunity to ask a powerful, obviously revered Mayan *brujo* to pray for me. I shook my head, wondering how I could have been in the holiest situation of my life and not ask for help when it was such an obvious thing to do. Apparently I was so lost in the love and beauty there that it was impossible to think of myself.

A few hours later, the surgeon unbandaged my hand and exclaimed, "How did you do it?" I looked down and saw that the finger looked alive again. The wound was healed. "Oh, I have a great surgeon!" I replied, laughing, too shocked to say anything meaningful. He responded with a tone of surprising gravity: "I did not do that. I don't have that kind of power."

Today as I write these words, I look down at the fine scar encircling my fingertip and remember the riches of love emanating from an ancient Mayan healer so poor that he burned his sacred incense in a rusty tin can. He was the most humble person I have ever been blessed to encounter, and my scar, like a little halo that I imagine shining over his head, will always symbolize for me the mysterious love of God at work in humankind, the great mystery of Christ in us. It keeps me aware of the death-and-rebirth cycles that accumulate over the course of a lifetime, and of the ultimate truth of Christian resurrection faith.

Through the years since then, my daughter, who is now a doctor, has told me about many minor miracles like my own and others much more powerful that she has witnessed in the hospital and that no one can explain. She says that friends always ask her what was her most exciting, horrifying, or bloody experience in the hospital. She wishes they would ask her what experience was the holiest.

Thinking about that day in Chichicastenango, I can feel again the inexplicable spiritual impact of the statue of Mary, the strong feminine presence and loveliness it portrayed. I have often visited the Cloisters in New York City to enjoy medieval statues of Mary that I love, but this one was different: she seemed to step out of it and come alive. Although I did not have a particular devotion to her at that time, something had moved me to recite the Hail Mary. It was not a conscious prayer for my injury to heal, yet there was undeniably a relationship between the powerful impression she had on me, the beauty of the Mayan healer, the love he generated in the little church, and the renewed flesh on my hand. Apparently the beauty of spiritual presence had opened my heart, and life-giving grace had flowed in.

This book originated in that experience, and the only point of my retelling it here is to wish you and your loved ones similar healing, or whatever you need that only God can give.

ONE
# The Mother of Jesus

ALL OVER THE WORLD, GLORIOUS POETRY, stained glass windows, sculptures, shrines, and breathtaking chapels have been created by artists such as Matisse, Chagall, and Michelangelo to glorify Mary and honor her memory. Where people are poor, colorful rituals honoring Mary on her Holy Days imprint the bleak cycle of the year with excitement, meaning, and joy.[1] In Eastern Orthodoxy, thousands of icons of Mary are often said to shine with the beauty of the divine energies. In the twelfth century alone, more than fifty soaring cathedrals in the new Gothic style were named for Mary, and to this day they draw millions of tourists each year to feast spiritually on the heart-stopping grandeur of a Chartres or a Notre Dame. Throughout the world, music composed for Mary and images of the Madonna brighten the darkness like living lights.

How many millions of Hail Marys and rosaries are said every day? Estimates vary from millions to billions, but it is said more than any other prayer from the vast global Christian treasury. Each year, some twelve million women and men make pilgrimages to Our Lady of Guadalupe in Mexico alone, and countless millions more travel to Marian shrines all over the world.

In addition to these many forms of veneration, we should honor Mary also as a mother of a human child who grew up at her side, receiving her love and tender care.

## TEACHING HER FUTURE TEACHER

How do you raise your child, how do you interact with him, if he is also the son of God, the Messiah of your people? That question must have always been present in Mary's mind, in one form or another, from the moment of the annunciation. and as you watch your baby become a boy with prodigious spiritual and intellectual gifts, and you see more and more clearly that he has been called to history's most extreme challenge, how do you teach good manners and correct his grammar, as loving mothers do? It must be almost impossible to understand that one's child is the long-awaited savior, even though Mary is told many times either explicitly or implicitly who Jesus is: first by Gabriel, the angel sent to invite her participation in redemption; and then by the prophet Simeon at the time of Jesus's presentation in the temple when he was forty days old. On that same day, the prophet Anna recognized who Jesus was. There is no question, of course, that Mary believed her boy was more God's son than her own; nevertheless, it was a question of being the only woman ever asked to do so much.

To say the least, it is uncomfortable to imagine Jesus's uneducated mother teaching her future teacher, but the truth is, a mother is inevitably her child's teacher, and her influence on him goes deep and lasts for a lifetime. Like all mothers-to-be, since the beginning of time and in every corner of the earth, Mary undoubtedly discussed the situation with her beloved cousin Elizabeth while they waited together for the birth of their sons, with her own mother, and perhaps with a sister and her grandmother, too. As the loving wife of a wise and sensitive man, she unquestionably discussed over and over again with Joseph the great issues of raising this holy child.

When Jesus was twelve, and his parents found him in the temple debating with learned men, it became apparent that he knew who he was. But it seems likely that mother and son had discussed this fact frequently and long before the temple episode.

How then to bring him up? Probably, when he was a baby and a toddler, she treated him with the same love and patience and forbearance that mothers innately have for their children. She bathed and swaddled him, fed him and sewed for him. She fixed and kissed his scratches and scrapes. She tenderly cared for him and was always present for her son. As Jesus grew older, she showed him how to feed himself, how to be well-mannered at meals and respectful of elders, how to behave with other children. Perhaps ingrained admiration for his mother led to the respect for women that he exhibited throughout his life, even daring to speak with a woman at a well, although the law forbade men to have public converse with women. Probably by her example as much as by her words, Mary taught her son to reflect before acting, to ponder things in his heart before making decisions.

While Mary was illiterate, she surpassed all women of all time in insight, wisdom, and faith. She could educate her son through the Psalms she sang to him and the Bible stories that Jewish mothers of her era usually knew by heart. Probably she expanded and explicated these stories to evoke insights and original thinking in her child. Perhaps she helped open his mind to the wonder of thinking and speculating and imagining.

Surely she taught him her beliefs and trust and faith in God. Especially important in Jesus's learning process was his mother's constant encouragement. She imbued him with her own gravitas, her quiet strength of character. She taught him to be responsible, most likely by example, but also by correcting him when he failed to live up to her standards and expectations. For instance, when he failed to meet the caravan after Passover and instead sat and debated with temple scholars, she rebuked him with a soft anger born of a worried mother's concern.

She helped him recognize injustice, as she herself had expressed it at the age of fourteen in her powerful Magnificat, and she showed him that it is right to feel angry about injustice and to battle it wherever it occurs. It would be many years before Jesus overturned money lenders' tables at the back of the temple, but perhaps there was a seed of his mother's teachings in that emotional moment. Somehow, probably because of her strong Jewish family tradition—all the convictions, experiential knowledge, and wisdom passed from generation to generation—Mary was able to teach Jesus to confront the power of others, be it spiritual, physical, or military, without fear and with inner calm and faith. How many times did she tell him Bible stories such as that of David and Goliath or Daniel in the Lion's Den?

We do not know exactly why God chose Mary to be the mother of the Messiah, but it seems fair to assume that her mind and spirit and soul reflected what God wanted to see in his son. A loving mother has a vast impact on her child.

The mother of Jesus was willing to spend and be spent in the journey of raising her child, and she is willing to do the same for us. Entering into a relationship with her is to learn for yourself that "there is no limit to the holiness one can attain through closeness to Mary."[2]

Ultimately, Mary is a model of how to live. one of the holiest and most human instances of this occurred at the Annunciation, when she was invited to give birth to Jesus. How better to show us the way than through her positive, welcoming response to the greatest challenge with which any woman has ever been presented? She knew it could not be easy or always joyful to be the mother of the Messiah, nor was it easy to find her voice when she finally spoke. On the contrary, it took tremendous courage to lift up her heart in trust and agree to an overwhelming destiny.

Mary's response to Gabriel was simple, yet majestic and overflowing with humble confidence in herself and in her God: "Let it be." That is all she said. Yet these words have become a hallmark for Christians because they speak volumes about her inherent wisdom—and the spiritual potential in every human heart.

Let us thank God that Mary shines over the sea of the soul. Let us pray with Pope John Paul II, who loved Mary and dedicated his life to her: *Totus tuus,* "all yours." Mary, I am all yours.

# TWO

# Following Mary's Footsteps Toward God

T O KNOW THE LIVING FAITH AND LOVE and beauty that is Mary's, to allow her to transfigure your image of yourself and your vision of the world, there is no better way than commitment to a daily spiritual practice. *Daily* of course means as daily as possible, since emergencies, illness, vacation days, and various problems can interfere. Only the angels' prayer is uninterrupted. What matters for us is to make the commitment.

In what follows, you are invited to celebrate fourteen of the most important, revelatory happenings in the life of the mother of Jesus. In these selections from the New Testament, symbolic words and pictures tell of universal truths, desires, and feelings, all of which you will find echoing in your own experience as you watch and pray with Mary.

## THE ANNUNCIATION

### Mary Is Invited to Become the Mother of Jesus

In the sixth month the angel Gabriel was sent from God to a city of Galilee named Nazareth, to a virgin betrothed to a man whose name was Joseph, of the house of David; and the virgin's name was Mary. And he came to her and said, "Hail, O favored one, the Lord is with you!" But she was greatly troubled at the saying, and considered in her mind what sort of greeting this might be. And the angel said to her, "Do not be afraid, Mary, for you have found favor with God. And behold, you will conceive in your womb and bear a son, and you shall call his name Jesus.

"He will be great, and will be called the Son of the Most High; and the Lord God will give to him the throne of his father David, and he will reign over the house of Jacob forever; and of his kingdom there will be no end."

And Mary said to the angel, "How shall this be, since I have no husband?"

And the angel said to her,

"The Holy Spirit will come upon you, and the power of the Most High will overshadow you; therefore the child to be born will be called holy, the son of God.

And behold, your kinswoman Elizabeth in her old age has also conceived a son; and this is the sixth month for her who was called barren. For with God nothing will be impossible."

And Mary said, "Behold I am the handmaid of the Lord; let it be to me according to your word." And the angel departed from her.

(Luke 1:26–38 NOAB)

It is March 25, within a few years of the year we call 1, and a 14-year-old named Mary—Myriam in Hebrew—goes out to graze a small flock of goats on a rocky hillside in Galilee. A typical Jewish girl of her time, she has dark brown hair woven into a braid that swings across her back as she runs happily up the hill. She is thinking about Joseph, a local woodworker to whom she is engaged.

Mary is as ordinary as her name and expectations. Marriage and motherhood lie ahead, and the hard life of the very poor. After the ceremony she will wear a long veil and move to a one-room house just like her parents', made of stone with an earthen floor and high-placed air vents admitting a bit of light. Like her ancestors for many centuries, Mary will cook over an open fire, sit on the ground to eat, and sleep on a thin mat. Her mother and grandmother have trained her well in women's ways of nurturing a family, tending to the sick and dying with home-grown herbal medicines, and helping in childbirth.

Mary is afraid, but the angel is beautiful, and he speaks to her in a soothing, tender voice. Quickly, she calms herself. The message is curious, inappropriate, as though it were meant for someone else, and she struggles with herself before she speaks. If you could speak to Mary, what would you say?

## PRAYERS

Hail Mary! Full of grace.
The Lord is with you.
blessed are you among women,
and blessed is the fruit of your womb, Jesus.
Holy Mary, mother of God,
pray for us sinners
now and at the hour of our death. Amen.

    *—Traditional prayer dating to the seventh century*

Accept, O Lord, all my freedom.
Accept my memory, my mind, and all my will.
Whatever I am or possess,
you have graciously given me;
I give it all back to you,
to be completely governed by your will.
Give me only your love and your grace
and I am rich enough,
and I ask nothing more.[3]

    *—St. Ignatius Loyola, founder of*
       *the Society of Jesus (the Jesuits), 1491–1556*

How wonderful is your love!
You looked at your fairest daughter
as an eagle focuses its eye upon the sun;
You, the eternal Father, saw
her radiance,
and the Word became flesh in her.[4]

    *—St. Hildegard of Bingen,*
       *German visionary theologian (1098–1179)*

Mary,
if I were Queen of Heaven,
and you were Thérèse,
I would pray to be Thérèse
so you could be Queen of Heaven.

    —*St. Thérèse of Lisieux, French mystic (1873–1897)*

 

## THE VISIT TO ELIZABETH

*Mary Visits Her Cousin Elizabeth While
Both Women Are Waiting to Give Birth*

Mary rose and went with haste into the hill country, to a city of Judah, and she entered the house of Zechariah and greeted Elizabeth. And when Elizabeth heard the greeting of Mary, the baby leaped in her womb, and Elizabeth was filled with the Holy Spirit, and she exclaimed with a loud cry, "Blessed are you among women, and blessed is the fruit of your womb! And why is this granted to me, that the mother of my Lord should come to me? For behold, when the voice of your greeting came to my ears, the [baby] in my womb leaped for joy. And blessed is she who believed that there would be a fulfillment of what was spoken to her from the Lord." . . . And Mary remained with her about three months, and returned to her home. (*Luke 1:39–45, 56 NOAB*)

The joy of Gabriel's message has barely subsided when Mary finds herself in a critical situation: she is pregnant and unmarried in an era when patriarchal laws make a woman in this situation an object of shame and shunning, possibly of death threats. Even Joseph, her fiancé, wants nothing more to do with her (Matthew 1:19). Isolated from everyone except God, she flees Nazareth in the hope of finding support and understanding from the one person she thinks will be compassionate, her cousin Elizabeth, an older woman who has the maturity to understand. So Mary rushes alone into the hill country where skirmishes between bandits and Roman soldiers are common and dangerous for innocent passers-by. But she is oblivious to the danger, and indifferent to the misery of walking in thin sandals over fifty miles of burning roads in the heat of May.

Can you imagine what this journey is like for her? Do you picture her feeling ill from morning sickness or other discomforts that may come in the first trimester of pregnancy?

In your imagination, watch as Elizabeth runs to greet her beloved cousin and welcomes her so jubilantly that Elizabeth's baby kicks for joy. Awed and overjoyed, she speaks prophetic words to Mary that will be repeated until the end of time: "Blessed are you among women, and blessed is the fruit of your womb." Elizabeth reveals herself to be a prophet. Imagine yourself speaking to Elizabeth. What would you say?

## PRAYERS

Mother of the Redeemer, with great joy
we call you blessed.

  —*Pope John Paul II (served 1978–2005)*

We greet you, holy Queen,
our life, our joy, and our hope,
Mother full of mercy, we cry to you in trust,
Exiled children of fallen Eve,
see our sighs and tears,
see our world of sadness.
Mother, plead for us.
Turn then towards us those eyes that plead our cause,
and when our life on earth is done,
show us then your Son,
blessed fruit of your virgin womb,
Jesus Christ our God.
O Mary, full of kindness,
O Mary, full of love,
O joyful Mary, full of peace and grace.

  —*A new* Salve Regina, *Mount St. Bernard's Abbey*

Hail holy lady, most holy queen, Mary mother of
God, chosen by the most holy Father in heaven,
consecrated by God with his most holy and
beloved Son and the Holy Spirit the comforter.
The fullness of grace and goodness descended on
you and remains in you.

  —*St. Francis of Assisi, beloved founder of the Franciscans
  (ca. 1182–1226)*

# THE MAGNIFICAT

*Mary Sings Her Great Song of Praise, "My Soul Magnifies the Lord
and My Spirit Rejoices in God My Savior"*

And Mary said:
My soul magnifies the Lord,
and my spirit rejoices in God my Savior,
for he has regarded the low estate of his handmaiden.
For behold, henceforward all generations shall call me blessed;
for he who is mighty has done great things for me,
and holy is his name.
And his mercy is on those who fear him
from generation to generation.
He has shown strength with his arm,
he has scattered the proud in the imagination of their hearts,
he has put down the mighty from their thrones,
and exalted those of low degree;
he has filled the hungry with good things
and the rich he has sent empty away.
He has helped his servant Israel,
in remembrance of his mercy,
as he spoke to our fathers,
to Abraham and to his posterity forever.
(Luke 1:46–55 noab)

Picture yourself standing beside Elizabeth on the hot afternoon when Mary comes into sight after her long journey. Now look at Elizabeth as she smiles and laughs and runs to embrace her tired young cousin. As she holds Mary, Elizabeth rejoices in Mary's deep identity and great calling, which has been revealed to no one but Mary and herself.

Unlike many of her friends, Mary has never thought of herself as an insignificant female destined for poverty and little else; she never accepted the saying that nothing good can come from Nazareth. But neither could she conceive of herself as a woman called to greatness. Now, however, in the mirror of the older woman's eyes, her self-image shifts dramatically. Seeing herself from Elizabeth's perspective—feeling *recognized*, feeling *known*—Mary sees herself as she really is.

Mary responds to Elizabeth's elated greeting with her own outburst of joy. In your imagination, watch and listen carefully as Mary almost sings the exquisite words of the song we name the Magnificat. What would it be like for you to hear this magnificent prayer spoken for the first time in history? When she finishes, what would you like to say to her? What does she say to you?

## PRAYERS

O, God,
help me to believe
the truth about myself—
no matter how beautiful it is![5]
    *—Macrina Wiederkehr, contemporary Benedictine writer*

*Alleluia!*
Praise God in his sanctuary;
praise him in the vault of heaven,
praise him for his mighty deeds;
praise him for his own greatness.
Praise him with dance and tambourines;
Praise him with pipe and strings;
praise him with clashing cymbals,
praise him with clanging cymbals!
Let everything that breathes
sing praise to the LORD.
*Alleluia!*
    *—Psalm 150*

O LORD, my heart is not proud
nor do I have arrogant eyes.
I am not engrossed in ambitious matters,
nor in things too great for me.

I have quieted and stilled my soul
like a weaned child on its mother's lap;
like a contented child is my soul.

Hope in the LORD, O Israel,
now and forever.
    —*Psalm 131*


O, Mary, mother of Christ and of the family of God, help us in our evangelical ministry. We think of you in a special way because of your perfect gratitude in the words you spoke when your cousin Elizabeth, the mother of John the Baptizer, called you "blessed among women." You never became complacent in your blessedness, but focused your thoughts on all women and men. Yes, you thought of everyone, but you had a special preference for the poor, the same preference that your son would have one day. . . . O Mary, lend us your voice! Sing with us! Beg your son to accomplish in us, in all their fullness, his father's plans.[6]
    —*Dom Helder Camera, Brazilian bishop and*
    *social activist (1910–2000)*


⌒


## THE NATIVITY

### *Mary Gives Birth to Jesus*

*In those days a decree went out from Caesar Augustus that all the world should be enrolled. This was the first enrollment, when Quirinius was governor of Syria. And all went to be enrolled, each to his own city. And Joseph also went up from Galilee, from the city of Nazareth, to Judea, to the city of David, which is called Bethlehem, because he was of the house and lineage of David, to be enrolled with Mary, his betrothed, who was with child. And while they were there, the time came for her to be delivered. And she gave birth to her first-born son and wrapped him in swaddling cloths, and laid him in a manger, because there was no place for them in the inn.* (Luke 2:1–7 NOAB)

It is December of the year we call 1, late in the third trimester of Mary's pregnancy, and careful plans have been made for the local midwife and women in Mary's family to help her deliver the baby. But dreaded news arrives, a message so important that soldiers of the Roman Empire have carried it on horseback almost a hundred miles from Damascus to Galilee. The imperial order states that a census is being taken, and everyone must register in person in his native town, which for Mary and Joseph means an eighty-mile journey to Bethlehem. They set out almost immediately, Joseph on foot, worried about his wife; Mary, heavy and uncomfortable, swaying on a thin donkey's back. Food is scarce, the night is cold, and the journey feels endless to them both.

Imagine that at a considerable distance before Bethlehem, Mary's water breaks, and she feels the first traces of pain. Labor has begun. Struggling to hide his fear, Joseph reassures her that Bethlehem is not far, and he will soon find a suitable place for her to labor and deliver her child. An hour passes before a searing pain sweeps across her body, announcing that contractions have begun in earnest.

The only shelter Joseph finds is a cold, dark stable by an inn, and he carries Mary inside. Anguish almost overwhelms him. Chances of both Mary and the baby surviving are slim. Does Joseph know how to deliver a baby? What kind of prayer is he probably saying? Perhaps he recalls Yahweh's promise in Isaiah 43:2,

*"when you pass through the waters, I will be with you."*

Hours pass, and at last Mary gives birth to a perfect little boy, her youth, strength, and faith having brought them both safely through the grueling day. Now the whole atmosphere in the stable is transformed: everyone weeps with relief and joy. Jesus the Christ is now in the world. Picture the love on Joseph's face as he tenderly places the infant on Mary's chest. Imagine Mary in this instant of bonding with her baby.

## PRAYERS

O True God,
I wake up today invoking your name and
    Holy Mary's,
for the running star has risen over Jerusalem,
and teaches me to say:

Arise in joy,
all you who love God,
daylight has come,
and the night has gone its way.[7]
—*Folquet of Marseilles, twelfth-century bishop*


Come, let us sing to the LORD,
let us make a joyful sound
to the Rock of our salvation.
Let us come before him giving thanks,
with music and songs of praise.

For the LORD is the great God,
the great King above all gods.

In his hand are the depths of the earth
and the mountain heights.
The sea is his, for he made it,
and his hand shaped the dry land.

Come and worship; let us bow down,
kneel before the LORD, our Maker.
He is our God, and we his people;
the flock he leads and pastures.

Would that today you heard his voice! . . .
—*Psalm 95*

～

## PONDERING THINGS IN HER HEART

*Mary Thinks Deeply about Profound Events*

*[T]he shepherds said to one another, "Let us go to Bethlehem and see this event that the Lord has made known to us." So they hurried away and found Mary and Joseph, and the baby lying in the manger. When they saw the child they repeated what they had been told about him, and everyone who heard it was astonished at what the shepherds said to them. As for Mary, she treasured all these things and pondered them in her heart. (Luke 2:15b–19 NJB)*

Mary is asleep in the run-down stable in Bethlehem where she gave birth to Jesus. Joseph sits on the ground on a well-worn mat close to his wife and to the small wooden manger that usually holds food for animals but today substitutes for a cradle.

Imagine the sound of people approaching. Startled, you look toward the large gate just as it opens, and a group of shepherds in patched, coarse woolen robes appears in the doorway. They tell you a startling story about an apparition of an angel who told them such amazing things about a boy just born in Bethlehem that they felt compelled to come see him for themselves.

Mary is standing up now, wide awake, pensive and silent, and everything about her reveals fulfillment and joy, despite her obvious exhaustion. Warm light in her weary eyes speaks of overwhelming love for her husband and her tiny son. Imagine that Mary invites everyone to kneel on the ground close to Jesus to pray. What is her prayer?

## PRAYERS

### PRAYER TO OUR LADY OF APARECIDA
(a title given to Mary as the patron saint of Brazil)

Lady Aparecida, a son of yours who belongs to you unreservedly—*totus tuus*—called by the mysterious plan of Providence to be the Vicar of your son on earth, wishes to address you at this moment. He recalls with emotion, because of the brown color of this image of yours, another image of yours, the Black Virgin of Jasna Gora.

Mother of God and our Mother, protect the church, the pope, the bishops, the priests and all the faithful people; welcome under your protecting mantle men and women religious, families, children, young people, and their educators.

Health of the sick and Consoler of the afflicted, comfort those who are suffering in body and soul; be the light of those who are seeking Christ, the Redeemer of all; show all people that you are the mother of our confidence.

Queen of Peace and Mirror of Justice, obtain peace for the world; ensure that . . . and all countries may have lasting peace, that we will always live together as brothers and sisters and as children of God.

Our Lady Aparecida, bless all your sons and daughters who pray and sing to you here and elsewhere. Amen.

—*Pope John Paul II (served 1978–2005)*

PRAYER FOR SPIRITUAL GROWTH

Dear Lord, you see how we become used to everything. Once I gladly took up your service with the firm intent of being wholly surrendered to you. But since every day brings nearly the same thing over and over again, it seems to me that my prayer has been circumscribed. I limit myself to just what seems necessary for the task at hand so that in the end my spirit has assumed the size of this small task. I ask you to help me not to narrow myself in this way; expand me again; give me some of the power of Mary's consent, which waits in readiness for the entire divine will, which is always as all-embracing as it was when first pronounced and which is daily conformed anew. She may have been glad or afraid or hopeful, weary of the daily work or led to the cross: always she stood before you as at first, accepting everything you said, hoping to do everything you wished. Behind every one of

your wishes, even the smallest, she saw the great,
unlimited will of the Father which you, the Son,
were fulfilling.[8]

—*Adrienne von Speyr, Swiss Protestant physician
and mystic (1902–1967)*

⌒

## SIMEON'S PROPHECY

### *A Sword Will Pierce Mary's Heart*

*When the time came for their purification according to the
law of Moses, they brought him up to Jerusalem to present
him to the Lord. . . . Now there was a man in Jerusalem whose
name was Simeon, and this man was righteous and devout,
looking for the consolation of Israel, and the Holy Spirit
was upon him. And it had been revealed to him by the Holy
Spirit that he should not see death before he had seen the Lord's
Christ. And inspired by the Spirit he came into the temple;
and when the parents brought in the child Jesus, to do for him
according to the custom of the law, he took him up in his arms
and blessed God and said:*

> *"Lord, now let your servant depart in peace,*
> *according to your word;*
> *for my eyes have seen your salvation*
> *which you have prepared in the presence of all peoples,*
> *a light for revelation to the Gentiles,*
> *and for glory to your people Israel."*

*And his father and his mother marveled at what was said about him, and Simeon blessed them and said to Mary his mother, "This child is destined to be the downfall and rise of many in Israel, a sign that will be opposed—and you yourself shall be pierced with a sword—so that the thoughts of many hearts may be laid bare."*

(Luke 2:22–35 noab)

It is February 2 of the year we name 2, and Mary's time of separation from society is drawing to a close. According to Jewish custom, she was religiously clean a week after giving birth, but thirty-three days of additional separation are required to complete purification observances. (Eighty days are customary after the birth of a girl.) Now that Jesus is turning forty days old, he can be brought to Jerusalem for a sacred ritual that has been celebrated by Mary's and Joseph's families for many generations. The couple will present their son to a priest in the majestic temple, the heart of their world, and offer two birds as a living sacrifice.

The tiny baby Mary holds in her arms will one day shake this temple to its foundations by exposing corruption, questioning priestly authority, assailing the whole religious establishment for abusing the poor, for animal sacrifice, for their very concept of God?[8] Surely no one could suspect that this innocent baby will be killed for revealing that God is love, and that the authentic temple of God lies in the human heart.

And yet, there is one person with the vision to see what lies ahead: Simeon, a living prophet, and he happens to be in the temple when you arrive with the holy family. Now a very old man, he approaches Mary. Simeon recites an exquisite prayer of perfect fulfillment and readiness now known as the *Nunc Dimittis* or "song of Simeon," telling God that his life's purpose has been fulfilled by learning that the Messiah has come in Mary's child.

How do you imagine Mary feels listening to Simeon's beautiful affirmation? Simeon echoes God's promise made on the holiest day of her life some ten months ago, when she became pregnant. Simeon's insights resound like a reaffirmation of that message for Mary to cling to should she ever need reassurance about her child's true identity.

Sadly, there is little time for Mary and Joseph to rejoice in the prophet's words, as he turns to Mary and prophesies extreme suffering. How does Mary look when she hears this? Does she believe Simeon? Does she remain silent? If not, what does she say? Would you like to speak with Mary, Joseph, or Simeon?

## PRAYERS

I rejoiced with those who said to me,
"Let us go to the house of the LORD!"
And now we have set foot
within your gates, O Jerusalem!

Jerusalem, just like a city,
where everything falls into place!
There the tribes go up.
The tribes of the LORD, the assembly of Israel,
    to give thanks to the LORD's name.
    There stand the courts of justice,
    the offices of the house of David.

    Pray for the peace of Jerusalem:
    "May those who love you prosper!
    May peace be within your walls
    and security within your citadels!"
—*Psalm 122*[9]

PRAYER TO OUR LADY OF COMBERMERE
*(a title given to Mary in Combermere, Ontario)*

O, Mary, you desire so much to see Jesus loved. Since you love me, this is the favor which I ask of you: to obtain for me a great personal love of Jesus Christ. You obtain from your son whatever you please; pray for me that I may never lose the grace of God, that I may increase in holiness and perfection from day to day, and that I may faithfully and nobly fulfill the great calling in life which your divine son has given me. By that grief which you suffered at Calvary when you beheld Jesus dying on the cross, obtain for me a happy death, that by loving Jesus and you, my Mother, on earth, I may share your joy in loving and blessing the Father, the Son, and the Holy Spirit forever in Heaven.

Our Lady of Combermere, pray for us.
—*Madonna House Apostolate, founded 1947 by*
*Catherine de Hueck Dougherty*


We place ourselves in your keeping, Holy Mother
of God.
Hear the prayer of your children in distress
and protect us all from danger,
O you who are so blessed.
—Sub tuum Praesidium, *the oldest extant*
*hymn to Mary*


⌒


## MEETING THE PROPHET ANNA

*A Woman Prophet*
*Proclaims the Greatness of Mary's Son*


*There was a prophet, Anna, the daughter of Phanuel, of the*
*tribe of Asher. She was well on in years. Her days of girlhood over,*
*she had been married for seven years before becoming a widow. She*
*was now eighty-four years old and never left the Temple, serving*
*God night and day with fasting and prayer. She came up at that*
*very moment and began to praise God; and she spoke of the child to*
*all who looked forward to the deliverance of Jerusalem.*
(*Luke 2:36–38 NJB*)

Picture yourself inside the spectacular Jerusalem temple with Mary, Joseph, and the infant Jesus. While you wait for the presentation ceremony to begin, observe a steady stream of people arriving at the temple with flailing birds, bleating calves, and other terrified animals to be sacrificed by blood-splattered priests as living offerings to Yahweh. In addition to presentation offerings, there are peace offerings, guilt offerings, thanksgiving offerings, and others. Mary and Joseph purchased two doves for Jesus's ritual.

As part of the rites of presentation, Joseph hands Jesus to the priest, who then gives him back. There is rich symbolic meaning in the gesture, suggesting that a child belongs to God and is only on loan to the parents for a time.

After the ceremony, an elderly woman renowned for her holiness comes over to Mary. She is the prophet Anna, and Mary is deeply moved to meet a woman of such *gravitas*, such depth and seriousness of purpose. Anna' prophetic gifts and character have been formed through half a century of widowhood made meaningful by her spirituality. As an elder, Anna has been allowed for many years to leave the confines of the women's court and go about the temple as she wishes, devoting her remaining time to worship. Sadly, her words are not recorded in the New Testament, but she knows in the spirit of prophecy who Jesus is. She sees, as did Simeon, that he is the Messiah. From this moment on, Anna will reveal to everyone who comes to the temple that the savior has been born.

Imagine that you hear Mary speak to Anna. What does she say? What does Anna say in return?

## PRAYERS

Some of you I will hollow out.

I will make you a cave.

I will carve you so deep the stars will shine in your
   darkness.

You will be a bowl.

You will be the cup in the rock collecting rain. . . .

I will do this because the world needs the hollowness
   of you.

I will do this for the space that you will be.

I will do this because you must be large.

A passage.

People will find their way through you.

—From "Mother Wisdom Speaks" by
   Christine Lore Webber


For your kingdom to come, O Lord,
may the kingdom of Mary come.

—St. Louis-Marie Grignion de Montfort,
   French mystic and priest (1673–1716)

⌒

# THE ESCAPE TO EGYPT

*Mary and Joseph Become Political Refugees to Save
Jesus from Herod's Killings*

*Suddenly the angel of the Lord appeared to Joseph in a dream and
said, "Get up, take the child and his mother with you, and escape
into Egypt, and stay there until I tell you, because Herod intends to
search for the child and to do away with him." So Joseph got up and,
taking the child and his mother with him, left that night for Egypt,
where he stayed until Herod was dead. This was to fulfill what the
Lord had spoken through the prophet:*

*"I called my son out of Egypt." (Matthew 2:13B–15 NJB)*

In your imagination set the calendar to nine
months before spring of the year 1, when Mary
is only a few weeks pregnant. Place yourself in
Nazareth with a deeply spiritual and sensitive
man named Joseph, a tanned, slender, rather
short woodworker who is hammering nails into
a wagon.

Joseph tells you about a startling dream he had
last night that told him to do exactly the opposite
of what he wants to do. He was about to break
his betrothal, even though betrothal is a binding
agreement, unbreakable except for infidelity.
But his fiancée is pregnant, obviously guilty of

infidelity, and that is cause for the radical act of ending the commitment. He is indescribably ashamed of Mary, yet cannot bring himself to ignore a dream, a source of divine guidance, and begins to feel he must go through with marriage.

Now, move nine months forward; it is early winter in the year 2, and you are in Bethlehem. Joseph is a married man with a newborn child, and once again has a powerful dream. This dream wakes him in the middle of the night with a terrifying warning to take his wife and baby and flee the house immediately, as King Herod's men are coming to kill Jesus. He instantly awakens Mary and tells her the horrifying news. She throws their few clothes and a little flatbread and goat's cheese into a satchel, pours water into a few goatskins, and the family rushes out into the cold night on a desperate journey to a foreign land. Robbers haunt the dark roads they will be forced to travel tonight. In the morning they will be safer on well-maintained Roman roads patrolled by soldiers. Way stations will have to meet their meager needs, since there is no money for meals or rooms at inns along the way.

Mary, Joseph, and the baby have become homeless refugees.

Mary has been driven out of her home, forced to leave behind her dream of returning to her home in Nazareth, her parents, family, lifelong friends, the community of women she talks with daily at

the well. Her entire lifestyle and support system are
gone. What would you like to say to her?

## PRAYERS

*Ti Prego*[10]

This season, Lord,
I feel like the dogwood tree,
Twisted, wind-whipped,
Frost-stripped,
Because the thaw came too quickly, Lord,
Too early—
Then the freeze.
The blooms hurt, Lord.
Trying to bud again
With tips ice-burnt,
Brown-burnt
Trying to feel spring, Lord,
Trying to feel, Lord,
Wanting to feel the bloom again,
        But when?
When, Lord, when?
Amen[11]
—*M. P. A. Schaeffer, contemporary American poet*

If you protect me, Mary,
your divine son will receive me
into the company of the saints

who walk with him in paradise.
I am like a lost sheep
    whose shepherd is searching for it;
    seek me, mother of mercy.
    Bring me safely home.[12]
    —*Raissa Maritain, Russian contemplative*
    *(1883–1960)*

Hail Mary of the Third World, full of grace, you who know pain, know the anxieties and the subhuman conditions of your people, the Lord is with you, as with all who suffer, who are hungry and thirst for justice, who know neither letters nor numbers.

Blessed are you among women, the women and men of the roads and pueblos, of furrowed faces, of brawny muscles, of calloused hands, of forlorn eyes—but with hope.

Blessed is the fruit of your womb, Jesus. Because without him, our life and the struggle for human dignity has no meaning.

Holy Mary, all of you holy, you are a thousand times holy, by your life, by the times that you carry water, that you smudge your face at the hearth, trusting and hoping in God, who has made you alone the Mother of God.

Pray for us, because it is the fault of our human egoism and envy that you, united with all poor women and men, suffer misery, totalitarian governments, economic repression, wars and blood and hatred.

Pray for us now, so that we change, so that there will be a vast conversion of heart, and all women and men everywhere will turn towards Jesus, our brother, your son. And pray for us at the hour of our death, so that the Lord will have mercy on those who have offended him in their brothers and sisters, the men and women of a world that is struggling desperately for life. Amen.

—*Latin American oral tradition, written down by*
   *Fr. Antonio Esquivel,* SJ

∽

## FINDING HER MISSING SON

*Mary Finds Her Twelve-Year-Old Son*
*Debating with Learned Men*

*Jesus' parents went to Jerusalem every year at the feast of the Passover. And when he was twelve years old, they went up according to custom; and when the feast was ended, as they were returning, the boy Jesus stayed behind in Jerusalem. His parents did not know it, but supposing him to be in the company, they went a day's journey, and they sought him among their kinsfolk and acquaintances; and when they did not find him, they returned to Jerusalem, seeking him. After three days they found him in the temple, sitting among the teachers, listening to them and asking them questions; and all who heard him were amazed at his understanding and his answers. And when*

*[Mary and Joseph] saw him they were astonished; and his mother said to him, "Son, why have you treated us so? Behold, your father and I have been looking for you anxiously." And he said to them, "How is it that you sought me? Did you not know that I must be in my Father's house?" And they did not understand the saying which he spoke to them. And he went down with them and came to Nazareth, and was obedient to them; and his mother kept all these things in her heart. (Luke 2:41–51 NOAB)*

It is a warm morning under a brilliant blue sky in spring of the year 13. Mary, Joseph, and their extended family are traveling home from Jerusalem with other Nazarene families after a joyful celebration of Passover rites and festivities. There are so many people, donkeys, and wooden carts piled high with provisions covered by billowing white cloths that Mary and Joseph's view of the full caravan is blocked. They are not aware that their twelve-year-old son is not with the group of boys who like to walk together.

In some ways, the scene resembles that of American pioneers in a covered-wagon train on the Oregon Trail in the nineteenth century. Jesus's family is too poor to own an ox, of course, and the ropes Joseph fashioned to strap down the wagon cover are made of reeds and rushes, rather than rawhide.

The caravan stops to eat. Jesus is expected to join his parents, but fails to appear. Mary and Joseph call him, but receive no answer, and send a boy to tell Jesus his family is waiting for him. But the boy comes back alone. "He is not here," the boy replies. What do you imagine Mary and Joseph are feeling? They rush up and down both sides of the caravan, calling out his name—"Jesus! Jesus!"—over the din of happy voices talking, telling stories, singing, and laughing. It begins to dawn on Mary that her child cannot be found. One minute terrified, the next minute trying to trust, Mary hopes he and his friends are playing a joke, but soon realizes that he is truly missing.

Mary and Joseph have no choice but to return to Jerusalem. An anguished day and a sleepless night filled with terror drag by before they reach the outskirts of the city, exhausted, wondering how they will find the strength to search the huge city. Public buildings and narrow streets still teem with pilgrims, soldiers, buyers and sellers, priests, women and children, plus the usual astrologers, snake charmers, wonder workers, and other charlatans who flock to the city at festival times.

The couple is almost beside themselves by the time they decide to begin with the temple. Jesus is so intent on religion and spirituality, so impassioned for God and learning, that he might have stayed in the temple, losing track of time. As they hurry toward the court of women where Joseph will have to leave Mary before he searches for Jesus, they suddenly hear voices enthusiastically discussing a theological point. Amazed, they recognize the sound of Jesus's voice, firm and clear, debating with the great scholars surrounding him.

Jesus, a boy on the verge of manhood, is oblivious to the pain he has caused his family. Picture Mary as she barges into the all-male group of scholars and interrupts their animated discussion with a rebuke directed at her son: "How could you do this to us!"

Jesus responds with a rebuke of his own: "Did you not know that I must be in my Father's house?"

## PRAYERS

The LORD is my shepherd.
I shall not want.
He makes me to lie down in green pastures.
He restores my soul
He guides me
in paths of saving justice
for his name's sake.

Even though I walk through the valley of the shadow of death,
I fear no evil;
for you are with me;
your staff is there
to comfort me.

You prepare a table before me
in the presence of my enemies;
you anoint my head with oil,
my cup overflows.

Surely goodness and kindness will follow me
all the days of my life;
and I will dwell in the house of the LORD forever.

—*Psalm 23:1–6*

Star of this stormy sea . . .
Turn your heart to the terrifying squall
in which I find myself,
alone,
without a map.[13]

—*Petrarch (Francesco Petrarca),
Italian humanist (1304–1374)*

O Mary, intercede for the children. There are too
many missing children; too many desperate children
orphaned in war; children made homeless by wild
storms, droughts, and famines; hopeless children
trapped in refugee camps; babies born addicted or
HIV positive. Help us to understand that the injustice
these little ones suffer is human-caused.

Hear our prayer to heal those who are indifferent: social structures, institutions, and leaders who
rule with swollen egos and empty hearts. Pray for
us, Mary, to not rest until every child is nourished,
healed, and freed from soul-warping hands. O
Mary, intercede for the children. Ask with us for
every infant to grow up loved. Help us to intercede
so that their eyes shine with love instead of tears.
Give us the grace to undo what the world has done.

—*Source unknown*

～

# THE WEDDING AT CANA

*Mary Intervenes to Help Inaugurate
Her Son's Public Ministry*

*There was a wedding at Cana in Galilee. The mother of Jesus
was there, and Jesus and his disciples had also been invited. And they
ran out of wine, since the wine provided for the feast had all been used,
and the mother of Jesus said to him, "They have no wine." Jesus
said to her, "Woman, what do you want from me? My hour has
not come yet." His mother said to the servants, "Do whatever he tells
you." There were six stone jars standing there, meant for the ablutions
that are customary among the Jews: each could hold twenty or thirty gal-
lons. Jesus said to the servants: "Fill the jars with water," and they filled
them to the brim. Then he said to them, "Draw some out now and
take it to the president of the feast." They did this; the president tasted
the water, and it had turned into wine. Having no idea where it came
from—though the servants who had drawn the water knew—the
president of the feast called the bridegroom and said, "Everyone serves
the good wine first and the worse wine when the guests are well wined;
but you have kept the best wine until now."*

*This was the first of Jesus' signs; it was at Cana in Galilee. He
revealed his glory, and his disciples believed in him. ( John 2:1–11 NJB)*

It is the year we call 30, and a gala wedding is underway in Cana, a village three miles from Mary's home in Nazareth. According to custom, the wedding party continues for seven days, with some guests remaining all week and others arriving throughout the week. Men and women come and go, festively dressed in special clothes reserved for weddings. Mary, perhaps a relative of the newly married couple, is talking and laughing with friends while Jesus and his small group of disciples enjoy a spirited discussion while drinking and eating on the other side of the room. Pungent aromas of roast lamb and spices mingle with the sweet fragrances of roses, anemones, and lilies.

Imagine that Mary overhears the head server whisper to the groom that the wine has run out. Watch as Mary goes over to Jesus to tell him there is no more wine, then instructs the servers to do whatever Jesus tells them.

Suddenly, the music and dancing stop, and exclamations of wonder and amazement are heard all over the room. Everyone is asking what happened. How is it possible that in the presence of a hundred reliable witnesses, water has turned into wine?

As the servers distribute the new wine, imagine yourself moving close to Mary so you can speak to her from your heart.

## PRAYERS

O *Mary*, you were promised in Eden as the woman who would right Eve's wrongs, the woman whose child would crush the serpent's head. Help us to conquer the evil that surrounds us everywhere, the physical, mental, moral, and environmental toxins that infect our homes and hearts, our workplaces and institutions. With the grace of your son, Jesus Christ, we can overcome these evil poisons through the vastness of your love.

O *Mary*, mother of Jesus the prince of peace, convert by his divine power, which surpasses all human power, the enemies of peace who ruin lives and destroy everything that is good. Bring to justice the dictators and tyrants and autocrats who illegally run dozens of the world's countries, daring to decide who lives or dies, who prospers or starves, who is jailed or goes free, as though they were themselves the God who created us all.

O *Mary*, win our hearts with your beauty so that we who want to do good in the family, community, and world will follow your way of faith and love, and be drawn to all the teachings of your son, especially his guidance to seek spiritual understanding before we speak or act. Conquer in us—and help us to conquer in ourselves—whatever resistance, inertia, or distractions block our good intentions.

Holy Mary *Conquistadora*, beloved mother of us all, we pray in deep gratitude for knowing you as a "conqueror," a woman of strength and courage who dares to take bold initiatives in the service of God's purposes. We honor you in this life with all our hearts and minds and will embrace you in the next, forever with all the saints, through the grace of your divine son, Jesus Christ, our Lord.

    —*Anonymous twentieth-century prayer from*
      *Latin America*


*Ave Regina*,[14]
holy, loving,
most noble queen.
*Ave Maris Stella*,
star of the sea and
moon where God took hiding.
But for you,
holy mother of God,
would the world have been lost.

    —*From an anonymous fourteenth-century*
      *penitential song*

～

## AT THE CROSS

*Mary Stands at the Foot of the Cross with Her Sister,*
*the Beloved Disciple John, and Mary Magdalene*

*Standing by the cross of Jesus were his mother, and his mother's sister, Mary*
*the wife of Clopas, and Mary Magdalene. (John 19:25 NOAB)*

It is mid-afternoon on a Friday in about the year 33, and the springtime sky has grown ominously dark, as though a devastating storm is threatening. A handful of people are gathered on the stony hill of Golgotha where criminals are frequently executed. But today an innocent man is being killed.

Several hours ago, the Roman authority in Galilee, Pontius Pilate, released from prison a highly prominent and popular young revolutionary named Barabbas who had been condemned to death for leading an insurrection against the Roman occupiers. In exchange for Barabbas, Pilate sentenced Mary's son, Jesus, a comparatively unknown leader of a small Jewish religious movement, to be crucified—an unspeakably cruel means of capital punishment intended to inflict maximum suffering. Jesus's small band of followers have fled in all directions in fear for their own lives.

Only four loyal people remain with the dying
Christ at the foot of the cross: his mother and three
of the closest disciples—Mary, the wife of Clopas;
John, the beloved disciple; and a woman who is
special to Jesus, Mary Magdalene. These few faithful people walked the way of the cross with Jesus
and for almost three excruciating hours have stood
by while the person they love most in the world is
slowly dying a horrific, barbaric death.

## PRAYERS

### LAMENT OF MARY

I am overwhelmed, O my son,
I am overwhelmed by love
And I cannot endure
that I should be in the chamber
and you on the wood of the cross,
I in the house
and you in the tomb.[15]
—*St. Romanus Melodos, Syrian hymn writer
first half of sixth century*

### THERE IS A BROKENNESS

There is a brokenness
out of which comes the unbroken,
a shatteredness out
of which blooms the unshatterable.

There is a sorrow
beyond all grief which leads to joy
and a fragility
out of whose depths emerges strength.

There is a hollow space
too vast for words
through which we pass with each loss,
out of whose darkness
we are sanctioned into being.

There is a cry deeper than all sound
whose serrated edges cut the heart
as we break open
to the place inside which is unbreakable
and whole,
while learning to sing.[16]

—*Rashani, contemporary hermit*

Hail Mary, full of grace, the Lord is with you.
Hail, hope of the needy, mother of those who no
longer have a mother. O Mary, when my heart is
full of grief, when my soul is enveloped in sadness
and fear, when emotions storm inside me, when it
seems that the gates of heaven have closed against
me and robbed me of my relationship with God,
to whom could I turn in my anguish but to you? O
blessed Mary, consoler of the afflicted and refuge
of sinners.[17]

—*Thomas à Kempis, German (1380–1471)*

⌐

## JESUS SPEAKS TO MARY
## FROM THE CROSS

*Mary Becomes the Spiritual Mother of All Disciples for All Time*

*Seeing his mother and the disciple whom he loved stand-ing near her, Jesus said to his mother, "Woman, this is your son." Then to the disciple he said, "This is your mother." And from that hour the disciple took her to his home. (John 19:26–27 NJB)*

For close to three hours, four anguished women and men have been keeping a deathwatch on the infamous hill of Golgotha under a heavy sky. They are the most loyal disciples of the holiest man who has ever lived, and they are crushed in mind and soul and spirit: his widowed mother, Mary; his most beloved woman friend, Mary Magdalene; the beloved disciple, John; and Mary, whose husband, Clopas, has fled with all the men, apostles and disciples, afraid of being arrested as accessories to Jesus's alleged crimes.

In ultimate contrast to the four great souls who would stand at the foot of the cross until the end of time if Jesus needed them there, several hateful Roman soldiers loll on the ground, playing dice as though they were bored. Soulless and indifferent to the suffering of the human being they nailed down three hours ago like carpenters making a fence, they may someday be spiritually awakened by the very men who have gone into hiding today. Those men are struggling to understand the divine tragedy that is underway on this "good" Friday afternoon, and in a few months they will be able to preach the gospel of love and reconciliation to the entire world.

## PRAYERS

As it was,
As it is,
As it shall be,
Evermore. . . .
With the ebb,
With the flow.[18]

    —*From* Carmina Gadelica, *Celtic prayers,*
      *Scottish Highlands, collected by Alexander Carmichael*

My beloved Mother, if you see something in me that does not belong, help me to remove it and to make you the guide of my life and all my power. I ask you to transform everything I find displeasing in myself, and to dissipate all darkness in my soul with the light of your faith. Take my self-centeredness and replace it with love. Take my arrogance and replace it with your profound humility.

Help me to learn to ponder things in my heart as you did when you lived on this earth; may I focus and concentrate without becoming anxious or distracted. May your continual vision of God inspire me to seek his presence every day. Transform my lethargy in the light of your heart's fire, and allow your virtues to come into being in my soul. Most holy and beloved Mother, may I have a spirit like yours, to know Jesus Christ and to praise and glorify God with love like yours, forever.[19]

—*St. Louis-Marie Grignion de Montfort*

O Mary, perfect disciple of Jesus, I come to dedicate my life and my priestly ministry to you. I desire to abandon myself to the will of Jesus, your son, and walk in faith with you, my Mother. To you I consecrate my life in the priesthood. I give you every gift I possess of nature and of grace, my body and my soul, all that I own and everything I do. Pray for me that the Holy Spirit may visit me with his many gifts. Pray for me, that by faith I may know the power of Christ and by love make him present in the world. Amen.

—*Source unknown*

⌒

## WAITING FOR THE SPIRIT

*Mary Prays with the Disciples in the Upper Room for the Spirit to Come*

*From the Mount of Olives, as it is called, [the apostles] went back to Jerusalem, a short distance away, no more than a sabbath walk; and when they reached the city they went to the upper room where they were staying; there were Peter and John, James and Andrew, Philip and Thomas, Bartholomew and Matthew, James son of Alphaeus and Simon the Zealot, and Jude son of James. All these joined in continuous prayer, together with several women, including Mary, the mother of Jesus, and with his brothers. (Acts 1:12–14 JB)*

Summer of the year we call 33 is quickly approaching, and it is a delightfully hot day in Jerusalem. Place yourself in the upper room in the circle of disciples seated around Mary. It has been only nine days since Jesus ascended into heaven, since the disciples lost the physical sight of the light in his eyes, the sound of his voice, the joy of conversing with him at meals. And yet the spiritual beauty in this blessed room is so palpable you can almost hold it in your hand. Look at the holiness on the faces and the grace in the postures, and listen silently. Notice that they are praying. In fact, they are deep in prayer, very close to God. It seems that

Mary, who has never appeared more beautiful or serene, is leading them in prayer. The words are so clear, it is as though they were speaking in a single voice. They are praying for the Spirit of the Lord to come to them, as Jesus promised.

## PRAYERS

Enter and penetrate,
O Spirit. Come and bless
This hour.[20]

*—Madeleine L'Engle, contemporary Anglican writer*

Lord, send your dew upon this sterile earth
and it will return to life.[21]

*—A prayer about Mary by Blessed Miriam Baouardy,
Lebanese nun (1846–1878)*

### PRAYER TO OUR LADY OF FIFTH AVENUE

I come to you, Holy Mother,
to ask your prayers for _____.

You give us all encouragement to approach you as your children, whose brother, your son, Jesus Christ, we claim as our blessed Savior and yours.

Help me now, I ask you, with a prayer to Him on
my behalf and for His sake. Amen.

> —*Prayer accompanying a statue of Mary and Jesus*
> *dedicated at St. Thomas (Episcopal) Church,*
> *Fifth Avenue, New York City, 1991*

*Sancta Maria, Ora pro Nobis!*[22]

Pray, O Mother, for all of us.
Pray for humanity that suffers poverty and injustice,
violence and hatred, terror and war.
Help us to contemplate with the holy rosary
the mysteries of God who is our peace.
So that we will feel involved
in a specific effort of service to peace.

Look with special attention
upon the land in which you gave birth to Jesus,
a land that you loved together
and that is still so tried today.
Pray for us, Mother of Hope.
Give us days of peace, watch over our way.
Let us see your son
full of joy in heaven! Amen.

> —*Pope John Paul II, in a sermon delivered*
> *on the Feast of the Immaculate Conception,*
> *December 8, 2002*

⁓

## PENTECOST

*The Spirit of Mary's Son Brings Sacred
Gifts of Wisdom and Speech*

*When Pentecost day came round, they had all met in one
room, when suddenly they heard what sounded like a powerful wind from heaven, the noise of which filled the entire house
where they were sitting; and something appeared to them that
seemed like tongues of fire; these separated and came to rest on
the heads of each of them. They were all filled with the Holy
Spirit and began to speak foreign languages as the Spirit gave
them the gift of speech. (Acts 2:1–4 JB)*

The last step of our pilgrimage with Mary finds
her on another hot day at the end of spring in the
year we call 33, again seated in the upper room.
Mary is deep in prayer, and her striking posture
is a living portrait of feminine wisdom in a spirit
set totally free. Her back is as straight as a cedar,
her head gracefully bowed, her dark eyes fixed on
a distant vision of something no one else can see.
Seated on mats close to her are women and men
from the earliest circle of Jesus's disciples, whom
she dearly loves.

The eleven apostles remaining since Judas's suicide are seated around a long table. Unusually excited, oscillating between joy and fear in anticipation of the monumental event that is coming momentarily, they are praying fervently. Imagine that you are there in the upper room, praying with Mary that the spirit will come quickly. What will this be like for the apostles? What more can happen after all the wonders and miracles of Jesus's ministry? Everyone in the room witnessed all kinds of "signs," one amazing healing after another, even Jesus's return from death!

As the hours fly by, those present find themselves praying more and more fervently, as though some invisible, pressing energy is building and reaching toward a crescendo. In your imagination, can you picture yourself there in the upper room praying with such anticipation? What is your prayer?

## PRAYERS

Mary, my dearest mother,
give me your heart
so beautiful, so pure, so immaculate,
so full of love and humility.
That I may receive Jesus as you did,
and go in haste to give him to others.
—*Blessed Mother Teresa of Calcutta*

O Mary, in your heart, I have found life.[23]

 —*Blessed Mariam Baouardy, Lebanese nun*

 (*1846–1878*)


 What shall I say to you, my God? Shall I collect together all the words that praise your holy name, shall I give you all the names of this world, You, the Unnamable? Shall I call You God of my life, meaning of my existence, hallowing of my acts, my journey's end, bitterness of my bitter hours, home of my loneliness, You my most treasured happiness? Shall I say Creator, Sustainer, Pardoner, Near One, Distant One, Incomprehensible One, God both of flowers and stars, God of the gentle wind and of terrible battles, Wisdom, Power, Loyalty, and Truthfulness, Eternity and Infinity, You, the All-Merciful, You the Just One, You Love itself?[24]

 —*Karl Rahner, twentieth-century priest and*

 *theologian, Germany*

# After You Read This Book

IT MAY HAVE OCCURRED TO YOU WHILE practicing the steps in this book that *The Way of Mary* resembles *The Way of the Cross* and *The Way of the Resurrection*. All three devotions consist of fourteen stations—although *The Way of Mary* calls them steps—that originate in the New Testament. The great difference is that the first two devotions focus on Jesus, while the one proposed in this book dwells on his mother.

The stations of the cross, or Via Crucis (pronounced "veea crutchis"), which appear on the walls of every Catholic Church, commemorate fourteen events from the day of Jesus's crucifixion. Throughout the year, but especially during Lent, Catholics walk the way of the cross in a church or garden, stopping at each station to ponder Christ's suffering and to pray. The practice may have originated in the first century. One ancient tradition holds that after Jesus's death, Mary would walk the path from the Garden of Olives where Jesus was apprehended, to the court of the high priest where he was tried, then on to the Praetorium for the confrontation with Pontius Pilate, and eventually to the hill of Golgotha. (See John 18:1–19:18.) We know that a few hundred years later, pilgrims were coming to Jerusalem from far away to walk the sacred path, sometimes on their knees in repentance for sins. The Way of the Cross ranged from only three stations during some eras to over forty at other times; only in 1731 did Pope Clement XII fix the number at fourteen.

It remains a mystery why a spiritual practice beginning and ending in Jesus's agony without any reference to the Resurrection was perpetuated for so long. But happily in the 1990s, a spiritual group in Italy, guided by a Salesian priest and scholar, Rev. Sabino Palumbieri, combined fourteen joyous events from the post-Resurrection season into a beautiful new devotion, the Way of the Resurrection, or Via Lucis (pronounced "veea lootchis"). These fourteen events are called "The Stations of the Light."[25]

It was my intention to suggest with this book that adding a Via Mariae to the Via Crucis and Via Lucis could bring a partial path to completion.

Together, the three "Ways" bring to life the full masculine and feminine beauty, majesty, and mystery of the Christian story, which the Via Crucis and Via Lucis alone cannot do. Completing the sorrowful Way of the Cross and the joyful Way of the Resurrection with the missing dimension of the sacred feminine is like restoring the original colors, sheen, and life to an ancient icon, or retouching a black and white film with color.

Today, the Way of Light is finding its way into churches and parish gardens in the form of uplifting pictures and sculptures; they bring into balance the suffering, evil, sin, and guilt depicted on the Way of the Cross with the faith, love, joy, and goodness of the post-Easter life of the risen Lord. If a formal Way of Mary were to be created and brought into relationship with the other two "Ways," it would surely nurture reverence for Mary and bring about increased devotion to Jesus Christ, her son, to whom she always points us, and of whom she always says, "Do as he tells you."

# Credits

Biblical citations were taken from *The New Oxford Annotated Bible, Revised Standard Version*, eds. Herbert G. May and Bruce M. Metzger, published and copyright © 1973 by Oxford University Press, Inc. New York City (indicated as NOAB); *The Jerusalem Bible*, copyright © 1968 by Darton, Longman & Todd Ltd and Doubleday and Company, Inc., published by Doubleday and Company, Inc. Garden City, New York (JB); and *The New Jerusalem Bible*, copyright © 1985 by Darton, Longman & Todd Ltd. and Doubleday, published by Doubleday, New York City (NJB). My preference for one translation over another depended generally on its fidelity to the original Greek or Hebrew. In some cases, the selection was based on the beauty of the language.

Psalms were taken from *The Christian Community Bible* © 1995 by Bernardo Hurault, published by Claretian Publications, Quezon City, Philippines, and by Liguori Publications, Liguori, Missouri.

I am grateful to Paraclete Press for permission to use "Prayer to Our Lady of Fifth Avenue," which appeared in Jon Sweeney's *The Lure of Saints: A Protestant Experience of Catholic Tradition* (2005); to M. P. A. Schaeffer for kind permission to reprint *Ti Prego*; and to Dorothy Walters for permission to reprint her poem

"What Is Happening?" from *Marrow of Flame: Poems of the Spiritual Journey* (Prescott, AZ: Hohm Press, 2000).

# Notes

1. In even the poorest cities of Mexico, for example, on December 12, the Feast of Our Lady of Guadalupe, people stand in line for hours to attend jubilant all-night masses where they can sing and praise and celebrate their beloved patron saint with unrestrained fervor and faith, for a few hours forgetful of their suffering.

2. This remark appeared in the Dec. 23, 2005 edition of *The Economist*.

3. Translator unknown.

4. Author's translation. See Hildegard von Bingen, *Lieder* [*Symphonia armonie celestium revelationem*], ed. by Prudentiana Barth, M.-I. Ritscher, and Joseph Schmidt-Goerg (Salzburg: Otto Mueller Verlag, 1969). The eagle here probably symbolizes the contemplative.

5. See Macrina Wiederkehr, *A Tree Full of Angels: Seeing the Holy in the Ordinary* (San Francisco: HarperSanFrancisco, 1988.)

6. Translator unknown.

7. See my book, *Spiritual Writings on Mary* (Woodstock, VT: Skylight Paths Publishing, 2005).

8. For a more thorough discussion of these ideas, see books by scholars in the Jesus Seminar, such as Marcus J. Borg's *Meeting Jesus Again for the First Time: The Historical Jesus and*

*the Heart of Contemporary Faith* (San Francisco: HarperSanFrancisco, 1994).

9. This psalm is part of the Little Office of Mary.

10. *Ti prego* in Italian is the equivalent of "I plead with you," or "I pray you."

11. Published in my book *Woman Prayers*.

12. See Raissa Maritain, *Raissa's Journal*, presented by Jacques Maritain (Albany, NY: Magi Books, 1974).

13. Translator unknown.

14. *Ave Regina* is Latin for "Hail, Queen"; *Ave Maris Stella* means "Hail, Star of the Sea."

15. Translator unknown.

16. Rashani, an Eastern spiritual name, gave this poem to friends before moving to a hermitage in an unknown location some years ago. She now has a spiritual center in Ka'alehu, Hawaii, the Kipukamaluhia sanctuary, where she offers retreats. See www.rashani.com.

17. See Thomas à Kempis, *Imitation of Christ*, translated by Ronald Knox and Michael Oakley (San Francisco: Ignatius, 2005).

18. See *Carmina Gadelica (Ortha Nan Gaidheal)*, vols. I–V, compiled by Alexander Carmichael, 1900–1954 (Edinburgh, Scotland: Scottish Academic Press, 1970).

19. Author's translation.

20. See Madeleine L'Engle with Carole F. Chase, *Glimpses of Grace: Daily Thoughts and Reflections* (San Francisco: HarperSanFrancisco, 1998).

21. See Chervin, *Prayers of the Women Mystics*.

22. *Sancta Maria, Ora pro Nobis* is Latin for "Holy Mary, pray for us."

23. Chervin, *Prayers of the Women Mystics*.

24. In this beautiful prayer, Karl Rahner, SJ, presses against the limits of language to describe the God of Jesus, whom he has come to know in contemplative prayer. See my book *Prayers for All People* (New York: Doubleday, 1995). The prayer was read at a 1995 Reformed worship service. Go online to www.reformedworship .org/magaazine/article.cfm?art.

25. See my book *Stations of the Light* (New York: Doubleday, 2005).

# ABOUT PARACLETE PRESS

## WHO WE ARE

Paraclete Press is a publisher of books, recordings, and DVDs on Christian spirituality. Our publishing represents a full expression of Christian belief and practice—from Catholic to Evangelical, from Protestant to Orthodox.

We are the publishing arm of the Community of Jesus, an ecumenical monastic community in the Benedictine tradition. As such, we are uniquely positioned in the marketplace without connection to a large corporation and with informal relationships to many branches and denominations of faith.

## WHAT WE ARE DOING

### Books

Paraclete publishes books that show the richness and depth of what it means to be Christian. Although Benedictine spirituality is at the heart of all that we do, we publish books that reflect the Christian experience across many cultures, time periods, and houses of worship. We publish books that nourish the vibrant life of the church and its people—books about spiritual practice, formation, history, ideas, and customs.

We have several different series, including the best-selling Living Library, Paraclete Essentials, and Paraclete Giants series of classic texts in contemporary English; A Voice from the Monastery—men and women monastics writing about living a spiritual life today; award-winning literary faith fiction and poetry; and the Active Prayer Series that brings creativity and liveliness to any life of prayer.

### Recordings

From Gregorian chant to contemporary American choral works, our music recordings celebrate sacred choral music through the centuries. Paraclete distributes the recordings of the internationally acclaimed choir Gloriæ Dei Cantores, praised for their "rapt and fathomless spiritual intensity" by *American Record Guide*, and the Gloriæ Dei Cantores Schola, which specializes in the study and performance of Gregorian chant. Paraclete is also the exclusive North American distributor of the recordings of the Monastic Choir of St. Peter's Abbey in Solesmes, France, long considered to be a leading authority on Gregorian chant.

### DVDs

Our DVDs offer spiritual help, healing, and biblical guidance for life issues: grief and loss, marriage, forgiveness, anger management, facing death, and spiritual formation.

*Learn more about us at our website: www.paracletepress.com, or call us toll-free at 1-800-451-5006.*

# ALSO AVAILABLE IN THIS SERIES